Welcome to The Rescue Farm.
    All of the animals here have been
saved from harm or just needed a new
home.
That is why we are The Rescue Farm.

Meet our first rescue Ms. Cluck,
a chicken.

Ms. Cluck lays eggs here at the Farm.

She is the "Mother Hen" of the yard,

loves to visit with everyone.

Meet our next rescues, they are rabbits.
Domino and Scooter.

They both love carrots and lettuce.

Of course Ms. Cluck is checking on
Scooter, cleaning and sharing his food,

making sure everyone is happy!

They share the yard with all
the other animals and of course Ms. Cluck

is right there checking on things.

Meet our next rescue. Ms. Henritta, a Turkey.

She likes to eat corn.

Ms. Henritta comes inside to get a snack,
along with Ms. Cluck.

Our animals love to come in the house.

She is our family pet and says
"Gobble Gobble".

Ms. Cluck cleans Ms. Henritta's house and visits her too.

You could say that they are friends.

Meet our next rescues, Jack and Little Man.

They are donkeys and they say "Hee Haw".

Little Man is the playful one.
He loves to smile and laugh.

Jack is a little older, all he wants you to do
is pet him.

Little Man also loves to have fun.

The donkeys need a large place to
run and play.

They like to eat apples and hay.

Ms. Cluck visits them cleaning and looking for bugs.

Meet our next rescue "Oscar",
he is a duck.

Oscar's favorite thing to eat is bread.

Oscar likes to share his pool with
Ms. Henritta the turkey.

You could say that they are best friends.

Meet our next rescues, Papa Pig and
Mama Pig.

They also need a large area to rest and
play in.

On February 10, 2019 they added 4 new babies.

Our newest additions to the Farm.

They like to visit and play.

And they like to eat corn and carrots.

Ms. Cluck even checks on them and gets her a drink.

Written By: Debbie Childree

www.ingramcontent.com/pod-product-compliance
Lightning Source LLC
Chambersburg PA
CBHW041613120626
46551CB00002B/423